everlasting blooms

beautiful arrangements and displays with dried flowers

fiona eaton

southwater

This edition is published by Southwater

Southwater is an imprint of Anness Publishing Ltd
Hermes House, 88–89 Blackfriars Road, London SE1 8HA
tel. 020 7401 2077; fax 020 7633 9499; info@anness.com

© Anness Publishing Ltd 1996, 2002

Published in the USA by Southwater, Anness Publishing Inc.
27 West 20th Street, New York, NY 10011; fax 212 807 6813

This edition distributed in the UK by The Manning Partnership
251–253 London Road East, Batheaston, Bath BA1 7RL
tel. 01225 852 727; fax 01225 852 852; sales@manning-partnership.co.uk

This edition distributed in the USA by National Book Network
4720 Boston Way, Lanham, MD 20706
tel. 301 459 3366; fax 301 459 1705; www.nbnbooks.com

This edition distributed in Canada by General Publishing
895 Don Mills Road, 400–402 Park Centre, Toronto, Ontario M3C 1W3
tel. 416 445 3333; fax 416 445 5991; www.genpub.com

This edition distributed in Australia by Sandstone Publishing
Unit 1, 360 Norton Street, Leichhardt, New South Wales 2040
tel. 02 9560 7888; fax 02 9560 7488; sales@sandstonepublishing.com.au

This edition distributed in New Zealand by The Five Mile Press (NZ) Ltd
PO Box 33-1071 Takapuna, Unit 11/101-111 Diana Drive, Glenfield, Auckland 10
tel. (09) 444 4144; fax (09) 444 4518; fivemilenz@clear.net.nz

Publisher: Joanna Lorenz
Project Editor: Fiona Eaton
Designer: Lilian Lindblom
Contributors: Fiona Barnett, Tessa Evelegh, Lucinda Ganderton, Terence Moore, Pamela Westland
Photographers: James Duncan, Michelle Garrett, Nelson Hargreaves, Debbie Patterson
Illustrators: Anna Koska, Nadine Wickenden

Previously published as *30 Dried Flower Displays*

1 3 5 7 9 10 8 6 4 2

CONTENTS

INTRODUCTION

Dried flowers used to be thought of chiefly as a winter substitute for unavailable fresh blooms. But improvements in the technology of preserving plant materials has resulted in an increase in types of dried flowers and the introduction of vibrant new colours. The astonishing range of materials and colours now available has heralded a new dawn of possibilities in dried flower arranging.

Today's approach to dried flower displays is to emphasize colour and texture by using massed materials so that the collective strength of their qualities creates the impact. Even where a number of varieties are incorporated in a display they should be used in clusters to realize the maximum effect. It is wise to avoid using individual stems of a particular material because this will make for rather bitty looking displays.

To get the best out of dried plant material, do not be afraid to integrate other materials with them, for example dried fruits, seashells and terracotta pots can add an extra dimension to a display. With all this choice, today's dried flower display is a far cry from the fading brown and orange dust-traps of the past.

Impressive though improvements in preserving plant materials may be, the ravages of time, sunlight, moisture and dust still take their toll on dried flowers. Do not make the mistake of believing dried arrangements will last for ever. A useful life of around six months is the best that can be expected before dried flowers begin to look dusty and faded.

However, by taking a few simple precautions, the life of a dried arrangement can be maximized. To avoid fading, keep the arrangement out of direct sunlight. Do not allow dried flowers to become damp, and be particularly

aware of condensation in bathrooms and on window ledges. To prevent the build-up of dust, give the arrangement an occasional blast with a hair-dryer set on slow and cool. When the arrangement is new, spray it with hair lacquer to help prevent the dropping of grass seeds and petals, but do not use hair lacquer on dust-covered dried flowers.

The book is divided into two sections. The first part, *Floral Displays*, presents a wide range of stunning dried-flower designs using varied colours, textures and shapes. The second part, *Special Occasion Flowers*, has wonderful gift arrangements, as well as ideas for Valentine's Day, weddings, including bouquets and church decorations, the arrival of a new baby and Christmas.

FIREPLACE DISPLAY

*This is one of the very best projects for a beginner. It is an extremely
simple design to make. Even though this display is for a fireplace,
turn it occasionally so that it fades evenly.*

MATERIALS

*wire cutters
chicken wire
basket
amaranthus
pink larkspur
pink and red roses
lavender*

1 Cut a piece of chicken wire
approximately twice the surface
area of the basket. Scrunch it up and
push it into the basket, filling the
whole of the inside.

2 Starting with the amaranthus,
push the stems into the basket,
through the wire mesh to the
bottom. Use this material as the
filler, and cover most of the top of
the wire mesh, leaving space for the
other flowers.

3 Arrange the larkspur in the
spaces between the amaranthus.
Stand back from the display to check
that the balance is correct.

4 Add the roses and lavender.
Make sure to put some rose
heads low down at the front of the
basket for added interest. Place the
display on the floor and check that
the balance is correct from all angles.

TIP

A fireplace display will tend to get
dustier than others. Clean with a
hair-dryer set on cold, and finish
with a soft brush. If some flowers
break with this treatment, you can
easily replace the damaged stems
without disturbing the whole display.

A SIMPLE POT OF ROSES

A simple rose pot display can be made in single colours or, as here, with a combination. Make a matching pair to stand on a mantelpiece or shelf for a symmetrical, formal effect, or perhaps add a fabric bow for a softer, more romantic appearance.

MATERIALS

knife
1 block plastic foam for dried flowers
terracotta pot
scissors
30 stems mixed roses
fresh moss
stub (floral) wires
wire cutters
glue gun (optional)

TIP

If you are using more than one colour, ensure that you have a good mix of hues over the display.

1 Trim the foam to fit the pot tightly and push in. Trim the top of the foam if necessary so that it is level with the top of the pot.

2 Trim each rose stem to the required length as you work. However, try to retain as much of the green leaf as possible.

3 Start in the middle of the foam, pressing in the tallest rose. Then work outwards, continuing to add the stems one by one. The roses should be at different levels so that the heads do not crowd each other.

4 Continue to press flowers into the pot. Finally, fix moss around the base of the roses with a glue gun. Alternatively, bend short stub (floral) wires to form U-shaped staples and push them into the foam to trap the moss.

CANDLE POT DISPLAY

*This beautiful arrangement of dried flowers in a terracotta pot is designed
to incorporate a candle. Contemporary in its use of massed flower heads,
the display has the stunning colour combination of deep pink peonies and
bright blue globe thistles surrounding a dark green candle and finished
with a lime green ribbon. It would make a wonderful gift.*

MATERIALS

*knife
1 block plastic foam for dried flowers
terracotta pot, 15 cm (6 in) diameter
wide candle
10 stems deep pink peonies
15 stems small blue globe thistles
scissors*

1 Cut a piece of plastic foam to
size and wedge it firmly into the
terracotta pot. Push the candle into
the centre of the plastic foam so that
it is held securely and sits upright.

2 Cut the peony stems to 4 cm
(1½ in) and the globe thistle
stems to 5 cm (2 in). First, push the
stems of the peonies into the foam,
followed by the globe thistle stems.

TIP
The effect of this display relies on
the peonies being tightly massed
together. Never leave burning candles
unattended and do not allow the
candles to burn below 5 cm (2 in) of
the display height.

3 Ensure that the heads of all the
flowers are at the same level.
Wrap a ribbon around the top of the
terracotta pot and tie it in a bow
at the front. Shape the ends of the
ribbon to avoid fraying.

SPICY STAR WALL DECORATION

This star-shaped wall decoration is constructed from groups of long cinnamon sticks. It is embellished with bunches of lavender to add colour, texture, contrast and a scent which mixes with the warm, spicy smell of the construction.

MATERIALS

15 cinnamon sticks, 30 cm (12 in) long
raffia
scissors
75 stems lavender
ribbon

1 Separate the cinnamon sticks into five groups of three. Interlace the ends of two groups of sticks to form a point and secure firmly by tying them together with raffia. Trim the ends of the raffia.

2 Continue interlacing and binding together groups of cinnamon sticks to create a neat star-shaped framework. Also, bind together the sticks where they cross each other, to make the frame rigid.

3 Separate the lavender into five bunches of 15 stems each. Turn the star shape so that the binding knots are at the back and attach the bunches of lavender to the front of the frame, using raffia at the cross points of the cinnamon sticks.

4 When all the lavender bunches have been secured, make a small bow from the ribbon and tie it to the decoration at the bottom crossing point of the cinnamon sticks.

TIP
For a Christmas look, substitute dried fruit slices and gilded seedheads for the lavender. Similarly, any sturdy straight twigs can be used instead of the cinnamon.

LOVE AND KISSES COLLAGE

This witty natural collage is made from tropical seedheads
and cinnamon sticks mounted on linen muslin. Even the frame has been
decorated with giant cinnamon sticks, glued over a simple wooden one.

MATERIALS

wooden picture frame
brown backing paper
scissors
linen muslin
glue gun
knife
small cinnamon sticks
florist's silver roll wire
heart-shaped or any other large
tropical seedheads
4 giant cinnamon sticks

1 Take the glass out of the picture frame and stick the backing paper to the hardboard backing. Cut the linen muslin to size, and fray the edges. Put spots of glue all around the edge of the muslin and then stick it to the backing.

2 Glue six short lengths of cinnamon into three crosses, and then wire them up to form a delicate metallic cross joint.

3 Glue the heart-shaped seedheads to the top of the picture; glue the cinnamon "kisses" to the bottom.

4 Finish by making a cinnamon-stick frame. Cut two giant cinnamon sticks to the same length as the frame and two to the same as the width. First glue a stick to the top of the frame, and then one to the bottom. Next, glue the side ones to these.

RED TIED SHEAF

A tied sheaf of flowers, arranged in the hand, makes an attractive and
informal wall decoration. To make a successful wall hanging, the sheaf
must be made with a flat back, while at the same time it should have
a profiled front to add visual interest.

MATERIALS
....
50 stems lavender
10 stems Protea compacta *buds*
10 stems natural ti tree
15 stems red roses
twine
scissors
5 cm (2 in) wide satin ribbon

TIP

The demanding aspect of the construction of the sheaf is the technique of spiralling the materials in your hand. But this display is relatively small, which simplifies the task.

1 Lay out the materials so that they are easily accessible, and separate the lavender into 10 smaller groups. Hold the longest protea in your hand, and behind it add a slightly longer stem of ti tree, then hold rose stems to either side of the protea, both slightly shorter than the first. Continue adding materials in a regular repeating sequence to the growing bunch in your hand, spiralling the stems as you do so.

2 When all the materials have been used, tie the sheaf with twine at the binding point. Trim the stems so that they make up about one-third of the overall length of the sheaf.

3 To finish the display, make a separate ribbon bow and attach it to the sheaf at the binding point.

EVERLASTING BASKET

Hydrangeas look fabulous dried, providing a flamboyant display that can simply be massed into a basket. They're also about the easiest flowers to dry at home. Just put the cut flowers in about 1 cm (½ in) of water and leave them. The flowers will take up the water and then gradually dry out.

MATERIALS

knife
1 block plastic foam for dried flowers
painted wooden basket
mop-head hydrangeas
globe artichokes
ribbon

1 Cut the plastic foam block to fit and fill the basket, and then arrange the hydrangeas to cover the top of the basket.

2 Add the dried globe artichokes at one end for texture.

3 Tie a ribbon to the handle of the basket to finish.

FLOWER CONE

This unusual design employs a series of stacked rings around a cone shape,
each ring containing massed flowers of one type and colour to create a
quirky display with a strong geometric pattern.

MATERIALS

1 plastic foam cone for dried flowers,
28 cm (11 in) high
galvanized metal container,
approximately 11 cm (4½ in) diameter
scissors
20 stems floss flower
40 stems pink roses
20 stems marjoram
10 stems small globe thistle heads
ribbon

1 Wedge the plastic foam cone firmly into the galvanized container. Cut the floss flower stems to about 2.5 cm (1 in) long and arrange a ring around the bottom of the cone to follow the ellipse of the rim of the container. Cut the rose stems to about 2.5 cm (1 in) long and, tight to the first ring, arrange a second ring with the rose heads.

2 Cut the stems of the marjoram and globe thistle to about 2.5 cm (1 in). Tight to the ring of rose heads, form a third elliptical ring with the marjoram. Tight to the marjoram, form a fourth elliptical ring with the globe thistle. Repeat this sequence of rings until the whole cone is covered. At the tip, fix a single rose head. To finish, wrap the ribbon around the galvanized metal container and tie a small bow at the front of the display.

LAVENDER BLUE

The heady scent of lavender makes it a perfect component for a ring to display in a bedroom, a bathroom, beside a window seat, or wherever there is a hint of romance. A smaller ring could hang inside a wardrobe or over a decorative coathanger.

MATERIALS

48–60 stems lavender
scissors
florist's silver roll wire
yellow rosebuds
strawflowers
blue cornflowers
yellow lady's mantle
yellow sea lavender
gypsophila
glue gun
1 twig wreath
satin ribbon
3 stub (floral) wires

1 Gather eight or ten lavender stems into a bunch, cut short the stems and bind them with florist's wire. Make six mixed posies with the other dried flowers, arranging the full, rounded flowers like roses, strawflowers and cornflowers in the centre and the wispy sprays at the sides. Bind the stems with wire.

2 Run a thin strip of glue along the stems of the first lavender bunch and press on to the wreath. Stick on more bunches of lavender, the heads of each successive one covering the stems of the one before. At desired intervals, add the mixed posies in the same way.

TIP

For the posies, which are to alternate with the lavender bunches, choose flowers in soft, complementary colours – blue, cream and green are ideal. If a glue gun is not available, fix the bunches and posies to the wreath form with stub (floral) wires bent into U-shaped staples.

3 Cut six equal lengths of ribbon, tie each into a bow and trim the ends. Cut the stub (floral) wires in half and bend to make U-shaped staples. Press five ribbon bows into the inside of the wreath and one on top. Glue on extra strawflower heads to fill any gaps or hide visible wires. Adjust the ribbon bows so they hang neatly and evenly.

DUTCH INFLUENCE

Inspired by the magnificent paintings of the Dutch Masters, this arrangement is composed in a painted and gilded wooden urn. A cluster of fruits – pineapple, grapes, and pomegranates – and a jug (pitcher) of wine complete the luxurious quality of the still-life group.

MATERIALS

*plastic-coated wire mesh netting
urn-shaped container
scissors
florist's adhesive tape
larkspur
deep pink, pale pink and cream roses
carnations
hydrangeas
long foliage
statice
strawflowers
lady's mantle*

1 Crumple the wire mesh netting and place it in the neck of the vase. Tuck in any stray ends. Cut short lengths of adhesive tape, twist them around the wire at intervals, and stick them to the rim of the container. When the design has been completed, the tape will be covered by the shortest of the flowers. Position the larkspur stems to create a fan shape.

2 Build up one side of the design. Arrange the roses among the larkspur stems. Cut the stems in graduated lengths and position some roses close to the rim.

3 Build up the other side in a similar way. Position the full, rounded flowers, such as carnations and clusters of hydrangeas, close to the base. This gives visual weight to the design. Add sprays of dried foliage to create a variety of texture, and to give the arrangement a more natural look. Finally, complete the arrangement by filling in all the gaps with statice, strawflowers and lady's mantle until it has a generous and opulent overall appearance.

DECORATED POT DISPLAY

*This display is purely for fun. The container is a terracotta pot decorated
with a painted head against a bright blue background. You can decorate
a terracotta pot with your own design and create a complementary
floral display for it.*

MATERIALS

*knife
1 block plastic foam for dried flowers
hand-painted terracotta plant pot
florist's adhesive tape
stub (floral) wires
reindeer moss
scissors
20 stems small globe thistles
20 bleached cane spirals
30 stems white roses*

1 Cut the block of plastic foam so
that it wedges into the decorated
pot and extends approximately 4 cm
(1½ in) above the rim. Secure it in
place with florist's adhesive tape.
Make U-shaped staples from the stub
(floral) wires. Tuck reindeer moss
between the sides of the pot and the
plastic foam and push the wire
staples through the moss and into the
foam to secure.

2 Cut the globe thistle stems to
approximately 10 cm (4 in) in
length and arrange them throughout
the plastic foam to create an even,
domed shape.

3 Cut the cane spirals to a length
of about 15 cm (6 in) and push
their stems into the plastic foam,
distributing them evenly throughout
the globe thistles.

4 Cut the stems of the dried roses
to approximately 10 cm (4 in)
in length and arrange them evenly
amongst the other materials in
the display.

BATHROOM DISPLAY

The starfish in this arrangement evoke images of the sea,
while the soft pastel colours – shell pink, apricot, blue, pale green
and cream – give it a soft summer look.

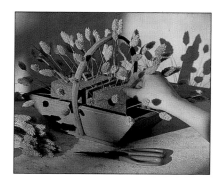

MATERIALS

knife
2 blocks plastic foam for dried flowers
pale-coloured wooden trug
florist's adhesive tape
scissors
50 stems natural phalaris
40 stems shell-pink roses
20 stems cream-coloured strawflowers
150 stems lavender
15 small dried starfish
stub (floral) wires

1 Cut the block of plastic foam to fit the wooden trug and secure it in place with adhesive tape. Cut the individual stems of phalaris to a length of approximately 10 cm (4 in) and push them into the plastic foam to establish the height, width and overall shape of the arrangement.

2 Cut the stems of the dried roses to a length of approximately 10 cm (4 in) and push them into the plastic foam, distributing them evenly throughout.

TIP
Although a steamy environment will cause dried flowers to deteriorate, if you accept the shorter life span, such arrangements will add an attractive decorative feature to a bathroom.

3 Cut the strawflower stems to a length of about 10 cm (4 in) and push them into the foam amongst the roses and phalaris, recessing some. Cut the dried lavender to a length of 11 cm (4½ in) and, by pushing into the foam, arrange it throughout the display in groups of five stems.

4 Wire all the starfish individually by double leg mounting one of the arms with a stub (floral) wire. Cut the wire legs of the starfish to a length of about 10 cm (4 in) and push the wires into the foam, distributing them evenly throughout the display.

DESIGNER TREE

Blossoming with strong primary colours set off by crisp white,
this indoor tree makes a natural link between the garden and the home,
and looks equally good in a doorway, on a windowsill, or a table.

MATERIALS

florist's adhesive clay
1 plastic prong
painted earthenware flower pot,
about 12.5 cm (5 in) diameter
modelling or self-hardening clay,
or plaster of Paris
straight but branched twig, such as
apple wood
2 dry foam balls, 7.5 cm (3 in)
diameter
secateurs (pruning shears)
statice
blue sea lavender
red broom bloom
red rosebuds
cornflowers
strawflowers
checked ribbon
dry sphagnum moss

1 Press a strip of adhesive clay on to the base of the plastic prong, fix it in the base of the pot and push a ball of modelling or self-hardening clay firmly on to it. Insert the twig and press the clay around it to hold it in place. Push the dry foam balls on to the twig.

2 Cut short the flower stems – the shorter they are, the fewer you will need to cover the balls and conceal the foam. Cover the first sphere with stems of white statice alternated with blue sea lavender and cornflowers. Fill any remaining gaps with extra flowers.

TIP
To give this display a lighter look, the terracotta pot was painted with white emulsion (latex) paint.

3 Cover the second sphere in a
similar way, using short stems
of statice close to the foam and
longer, wispy red flowers to provide
a softer outline. Position a few rosebuds and strawflowers at intervals
among the statice. Tie a ribbon bow
just below the higher ball. To finish,
tie more ribbons close to the pot, to
trail over the rim. Instead of a multi-
coloured check design, narrow ribbon
or tape in each of the three principal
flower colours may be used. Cover
the holding material in the pot with
dry moss.

ROSE AND LAVENDER POSY

*A bouquet always makes a welcome gift, but a bunch of carefully selected
and beautifully arranged dried flowers will long outlast fresh blooms,
to become an enduring reminder of a happy occasion.*

MATERIALS

*stub (floral) wires
12 large artificial or glycerined leaves
florist's (stem-wrap) tape
1 bunch lavender
1 bunch rosebuds
florist's silver roll wire (optional)
paper ribbon*

1 Fold a stub (floral) wire one-third of the way along its length, to form a 15 cm (6 in) stalk. Attach a leaf to the top by its stalk, and bind in place with florist's (stem-wrap) tape, pulling and wrapping the tape down to the end of the wire. Repeat the process with all 12 leaves.

2 Divide the lavender into several small bunches. Hold them together loosely, setting the bunches at an angle to give a good shape. This will form the basic structure of the posy.

3 Taking a single rosebud at a time, push the stems into the lavender, spacing them out evenly.

4 If desired, bind the posy with florist's silver roll wire so it will keep its shape while you work. Then edge the posy with the wire-mounted leaves. Bind in place again.

5 Unravel the paper ribbon and use to bind all the stalks together tightly, covering the wire and the stalks completely. Finish off by tying the ends of the ribbon into a bow.

WALL HANGING SHEAF

The rustic charm of this delightful hand-tied sheaf is difficult to resist especially since it is so easy to make once you have mastered the ever-useful stem-spiralling technique.

MATERIALS

1 bunch linseed
1 bunch white strawflowers
10 stems carthamus
8 stems large orange-dyed globe thistles
10 stems green amaranthus (straight)
twine
scissors
green paper ribbon

TIP

The sheaf shape makes a feature of the stems as well as the blooms. Finished with a green ribbon, this decoration would look lovely hung in a country-style kitchen.

1 Set out the materials so that they are easily accessible. Divide each of the bunches of linseed and strawflowers into 10 smaller bunches. Break off the side shoots from the main stems of the carthamus and the globe thistles to increase the number of individual stems available. Take the longest stem of amaranthus in your hand and, to either side of it, add a stem of carthamus and a bunch of linseed, making sure all the material is slightly shorter than the amaranthus. The stems of the materials should be spiralled as they are added. Add materials to the bunch to maintain a visual balance between the bold forms of the globe thistles and strawflowers and the more delicate linseed and carthamus.

2 When all the materials have been incorporated, tie with twine at the binding point. Trim the ends of the stems.

3 Make a paper ribbon bow and attach it to the sheaf at the binding point with its tails pointing towards the flower heads.

SPICY POMANDER

*Pomanders were originally nature's own air fresheners. The traditional
orange pomanders are fairly tricky to do, because the critical drying
process can so easily go wrong, leading to mouldy oranges. This one
made of cloves and cardamom pods avoids the problem, and makes a
refreshing change in soft, muted colours.*

MATERIALS

cloves
1 dry foam ball, 7.5 cm (3 in) diameter
glue gun
green cardamom pods
raffia
1 stub (floral) wire

1 Start by making a single line of cloves all around the ball's circumference. Make another one in the other direction, so you have divided the ball into quarters.

2 Make a line of cloves on both sides of original lines to create broad bands of cloves quartering the ball.

3 Starting at the top of the first quarter, glue cardamom pods over the foam, methodically working in rows to create a neat effect. Repeat on the other three quarters.

4 Tie a bow in the centre of a length of raffia. Pass a stub (floral) wire through the knot and twist the ends together.

5 Fix the bow to the top of the ball using the stub (floral) wire. Join the two loose ends in a knot to hang the pomander.

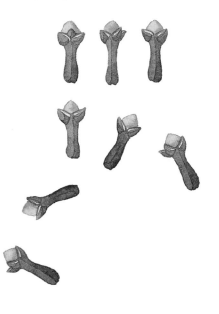

TRADITIONAL TIERED BASKET

This regimented formal design can be very effective and is one of the easiest for beginners to perfect. So long as you make sure that each layer of materials is the correct height, you should make a dramatic display, the loose and flowing ingredients combining well within the confines of a disciplined structure.

MATERIALS

knife
1 block plastic foam for dried flowers
rectangular basket
wheat
stub (floral) wires
lavender
roses
fresh moss
scissors or cutters

1 Cut the dry foam block to fill the basket and press firmly in. Start in the centre of the foam with the wheat, the tallest ingredient, wired into bunches of 8–10 stems. Pack the stems closely together to achieve a good density. Check that the height of the wheat balances with the basket size.

2 Wire the lavender into small bunches of 5–6 stems and push them into the foam directly in front of the wheat. Arrange the stems so that the lavender flowers come to just below the heads of wheat. Make sure the flowers are all facing the same way to achieve a symmetry.

3 Add the roses next, positioning them in front of the lavender. Add the stems individually, and try to keep as much foliage as space will allow. Place the roses at slightly varying heights to ensure that each flower head is visible.

4 Complete the display by covering the foam at the base with moss. Fix this in place with stub (floral) wires bent into U-shaped staples. Fresh moss shrinks a little when it dries, so allow it to overhang the sides of the basket at this stage.

Peony And Apple Table Arrangement

This delicate arrangement can be made for a specific occasion and kept to be used again and again, whenever a special arrangement is called for. The construction of the decoration is relatively simple, involving the minimum of wiring.

Materials

knife
1 block plastic foam for dried flowers
terracotta bowl
florist's adhesive tape
scissors
10 stems preserved (dried) eucalyptus
18 slices preserved (dried) apple
stub (floral) wires
2 large heads hydrangea
10 stems pale pink peonies
20 stems deep pink roses
20 peony leaves
10 stems ti tree

1 Cut the block of plastic foam so that it wedges into the bowl and secure it in place with the florist's adhesive tape. Cut the eucalyptus stems to about 13 cm (5 in), making sure that the cut ends are clean of leaves, and arrange them evenly around the plastic foam to create a domed foliage outline to the display.

2 Group the slices of preserved (dried) apple into threes and double leg mount them with stub (floral) wires. Push the six groups of wired apple slices into the foam, distributing them evenly throughout the display.

3 Break each hydrangea head into three smaller florets and push them into the foam, distributing them evenly throughout the display, and recessing them slightly as you work.

4 Cut the stems of the peonies to approximately 12 cm (4¾ in) in length and arrange them evenly throughout the display. This time, the peonies should not be recessed.

5 Cut the dried rose stems to
approximately 12 cm (4¾ in) in
length and push them into the plastic
foam throughout the other materials.

6 Arrange the dried peony leaves
evenly amongst the flowers. Cut
the ti tree into stems of approximately
12 cm (4¾ in) in length and distribute
them throughout the display.

AUTUMN ROSE BUNDLE

Roses, especially yellow or orange ones, will keep their colour for a very
long time, so this makes an ideal display to fill a dark corner.
For a smarter look, the arrangement could be trimmed with a fabric bow.

MATERIALS

1 cylinder plastic foam for
dried flowers
brown paper
glue gun
craft knife or scalpel
stub (floral) wires
pliers
scissors
12 stems orange or yellow roses
4 cobra leaves
raffia
fresh moss

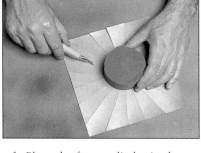

1 Place the foam cylinder in the centre of the brown paper and glue it in place. Cut from the edge of the foam to the outer edge of the paper, working all the way around at roughly 1 cm (½ in) intervals.

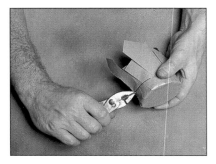

2 Fold the paper strips up to wrap the foam. Wrap a stub (floral) wire round the paper and the foam, making sure all the paper strips are straight at the base, and twist the two ends of the wire tightly together.

3 Trim the paper in line with the top of the foam. Cut the rose stems, retaining as many leaves as possible. Starting in the centre, push them carefully into the foam.

4 Wrap three to four cobra leaves around the base, fixing each one in place with a U-shaped staple made from a bent stub (floral) wire.

5 Wrap a stub (floral) wire around the leaves at the same level as the U-shaped staples and twist the ends tightly together to make a secure fixing. Trim the leaves at the base of the display with scissors, so that it will stand evenly.

6 Tie raffia round the base, covering all the fixings, and finish with a bow or a simple knot. If the roses had a limited number of leaves, fill the spaces around the stems with moss, to hide the foam.

AUTUMNAL ORANGE DISPLAY

*Warm autumn colours dominate this display both in the flowers and the
container. The lovely bulbous terracotta pot is a feature of the display, and
the arrangement is domed to reflect the roundness of the container.*

MATERIALS

3 blocks plastic foam for dried flowers
terracotta pot, 30 cm (12 in) high
florist's adhesive tape
10 stems glycerined adiantum
stub (floral) wires
9 dried split oranges
scissors
10 stems carthamus
10 stems orange-dyed globe thistles
10 stems bottlebrush

1 Pack the blocks of plastic foam
into the terracotta pot and secure
in place with florist's adhesive tape.
The surface of the foam should be
4 cm (1¼ in) above the pot's rim.

2 Create a low domed outline with
foliage using the adiantum stems
at a length of about 25 cm (10 in).
Wire the dried oranges with stub
(floral) wire.

3 Bend down the wires projecting
from the bases of the oranges
and twist together. Arrange the
oranges throughout the adiantum
using their wire stems.

4 Cut the carthamus stems to
approximately 25 cm (10 in) and
push them into the plastic foam
throughout the display to reinforce
the height, width and overall shape.

5 Cut the globe thistle and bottlebrush stems to a length of
approximately 25 cm (10 in) and
push them into the foam evenly
throughout the display.

SPICE TOPIARY

Fashion a delightfully aromatic, culinary topiary from cloves and star anise, put it in a terracotta pot decorated with cinnamon sticks and top with a cinnamon-stick cross. Sticking all the cloves into the florist's foam is both easy to do and wonderfully therapeutic.

MATERIALS

*small "long Tom" terracotta
flowerpot
knife
cinnamon sticks
glue gun
1 plastic foam cone for dried flowers,
23 cm (9 in) tall
1 small plastic foam cone
stub (floral) wires
large pack of star anise
cloves*

TIP

This lovely topiary would make an ideal gift – perhaps as a house-warming present, or for someone who loves cooking.

1 Prepare the pot by cutting the cinnamon sticks to the length of the pot and gluing them in position. Trim the top of the larger cone. Cut the smaller cone to fit inside the pot.

2 Put four stub (floral) wires upright in the pot so they project above the foam. Use these wires to stake the trimmed cone on top of the foam-filled pot.

3 Sort out all the complete star anise from the pack, plus any that are almost complete – you'll need about 20 in all. Wire these up by passing a wire over the front in one direction, and another wire over the front in another direction to make a cross of wires. Twist the wires together at the back and trim to about 1 cm (½ in).

4 Start by arranging the star anise in rows down the cone – about three each side to quarter the cone. Put two vertically between each line. Next, just fill the whole remaining area of cone with cloves, packing them tightly so none of the foam shows through.

5 Glue two short pieces of cinnamon stick into a cross. Wire this up, and use it to decorate the top of the topiary.

VALENTINE DECORATION IN A BOX

This display, in a heart-shaped box, demonstrates that dried flowers and seedheads look very striking and attractive when massed in groups of one type. Filled with romantic roses and scented lavender, this display can be made as a gift for Valentine's Day or simply as a treat for yourself. It can also be made at any other time of year using a different shaped box.

MATERIALS

1 block plastic foam for dried flowers
knife
heart-shaped box
scissors
1 bunch red roses
2 bunches lavender
2 bunches poppy seedheads
1 bunch Nigella orientalis

1 Stand the block of plastic foam on its end and carefully slice in half down its length with a knife. Then shape both pieces, using the box as a template, so that they will each fit into one half of the box. Fit these two halves into the heart-shaped box, ensuring that they fit snugly.

2 Divide the heart shape into quarters, separating each section by a line of the materials to be used. Fill one quarter with rose heads, one with lavender, one with poppy seedheads and the last with *Nigella orientalis*. Make sure that all the material heads are at the same level.

TIP

This arrangement is easy to make, but for the best effect do not scrimp on materials. The flower heads need to be massed together very tightly to hide the foam.

VALENTINE POT POURRI

This is a wonderful way of making use of spare flower pieces from other displays. This is not so long-lasting as pot pourri made the traditional way, but it's a quick and effective method when time is short.

box
red and pink rosebuds, or any suitable
assortment
lavender
scissors
reindeer moss
rose or lavender essential oil

TIP

The plain cardboard box used for this mixture has been covered with a broad red ribbon, and a piece of the same ribbon has been cut in half to create the decoration on the top of the box. Essential oil will discolour the materials in the box over a period of time. To avoid this, let the essential oil drops fall only on to the moss; with the lid closed the gentle perfume will still be imparted to the flowers.

1 Line the bottom of the box with rosebuds and a few stems of lavender. Trim the stems of the lavender fairly short, using mostly the flower heads.

2 Place some of the reindeer moss in the box, around the rosebuds and flower heads.

3 Trim the heads from the stems of all the remaining flowers and arrange them in the box. Add a few fresh flower heads if you wish, but make sure they are not too woody, otherwise they won't dry out.

4 Gently drizzle a few drops of the essential oil over the reindeer moss, to give the flowers a pleasantly gentle perfume.

HORSESHOE BABY GIFT

What could be nicer for new parents than to receive a floral symbol of good luck on the birth of their baby? The whites and pale green of this horseshoe make it a perfect gift or decoration for the nursery.

MATERIALS

14 stems white roses
42 stems bleached honesty
60 stems natural phalaris
scissors
silver wire
florist's (stem-wrap) tape
stub (floral) wires
ribbon

1 Cut the rose stems, honesty stems and phalaris to approximately 2.5 cm (1 in) long. Double leg mount the roses individually on silver wire, then tape. Double leg mount the phalaris heads in groups of five on silver wire, and the honesty in clusters of three also on silver wire. Tape each individual group.

2 Make a stay wire approximately 30 cm (12 in) long from stub (floral) wire on which the horseshoe will be built.

3 Form three small bows about 4 cm (1½ in) wide from the ribbon and bind them at their centres with silver wire. Cut a 30 cm (12 in) length of ribbon and double leg mount both ends separately with silver wire. This will form the handle for the horseshoe.

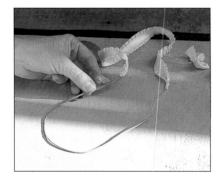

4 Make a horseshoe shape with the stay wire. Tape one wired end of the ribbon to one end of the stay wire. Tape one of the bows over the junction of the ribbon and stay wire, making sure it is securely in place.

5 Starting at the bow, tape the flowers and foliage to the stay wire, to its mid point, following this repeating sequence: phalaris, rose, honesty. Tape a bow at the centre and tape the last bow and the last ribbon end to the other end of the stay wire. Work the flowers using the same sequence back to the centre point of the horseshoe.

BRIDESMAID'S POMANDER

*Popular in Victorian England, traditional, sweet-smelling pomanders
make an interesting adornment for bridesmaids. This uncomplicated
version is built around a plastic foam ball, using head-to-head roses
interspersed with eucalyptus.*

MATERIALS

*stub (floral) wire
1 plastic foam ball for dried flowers
red ribbon
scissors
red roses
glue gun
glycerined eucalyptus*

1 Bend a long stub (floral) wire in
half and push the wire ends into
the foam until both ends protrude,
and there is only a little metal loop
left at the other end. Now bend the
wire ends back and pull them back
into the ball.

2 Attach a length of ribbon
securely to the loop end. Remove
all the rose heads from their stems.

3 Using a glue gun, place a drop
of glue on the underside of the
rose heads and stick the heads to the
plastic foam ball.

4 Begin by making a circle of roses
all around the middle, working
from top to bottom.

5 Now turn the pomander 90
degrees and stick another row of
roses down the centre, dividing the
pomander into quarters.

6 Fill in the quarters with the remaining rose heads, and then begin to insert small pieces of eucalyptus between the rose heads to hide any holes.

7 Take the two ends of the ribbon and tie a knot to the required length. If a small child is to carry the pomander, do not make the handle too long. Finish with a bow.

SUMMER WEDDING PEW END

A collection of these set high on the ends of the church pews produces
a dramatic effect, especially if all the candles are burning. These pew ends
can be made without the candle, and in a range of different sizes.
Keep the stems fairly long to give a balanced shape to the finished piece.

MATERIALS

2 canes 60 cm (24 in) long
40-45 cm (16-18 in) candle
florist's adhesive tape
pink larkspur
pink roses
stub (floral) wires
raffia
scissors

1 Place a cane on either side of the base of the candle. Hold them in place with florist's adhesive tape. Make sure the canes are firmly taped in place as tightly as possible.

2 Arrange a layer of flowers around the candle, with the heads just above the height of the tape fixing, holding them in place. Add more material to create a large posy with the candle in the middle.

3 Criss-cross the stems, at an outward angle, to produce a wide, circular display. Tie a stub (floral) wire around the stems and fix it firmly. Tie a raffia bow around the middle to cover the wire and attach a strong S-shaped wire at the back to attach the pew end to the fixing on the church pew.

TIP

When making a large display from a fairly small amount of material, the trick is constantly to criss-cross the stems as the display is built up.

BRIDAL BOUQUET

*The romance of roses, the veil-like quality of gypsophila and the luxury of
Singapore orchids are gathered together in this bouquet that could be
carried by the bride or her attendants, and then kept as a memento
of the happy day.*

MATERIALS

*scissors
pastel-mauve dyed sea lavender
stub (floral) wires
florist's silver roll wire
wire cutters
white florist's (stem wrap) tape
hydrangea
gypsophila
Singapore orchids
cream roses
purple statice
lady's mantle
strawflowers
pampas leaves
broom sprays
4 cm (1½ in) wide satin ribbon in
two toning colours*

1 Cut short sprays of sea lavender. Place a stub (floral) wire close against the stems and bind with silver roll wire. Bind the stems and false wire stem with florist's (stem wrap) tape. Bind clusters of hydrangea bracts, gypsophila and short-stemmed roses in a similar way.

2 Gather together several flower sprays and foliage stems and arrange them in one hand so that they cascade in a natural, easy way. Rearrange until the combination is pleasing, then bind the group of false stems together with silver roll wire.

3 Add more wired and bound stems to the group, a few at a time. Alternate the full, round shapes of roses and strawflowers with wispy sprays of gypsophila and lady's mantle. Bind the bunch of false stems with ribbon, overlapping each twist all the way down. To finish, tie more ribbons around the handle to create large bows with long, trailing ends.

TIP

To avoid crushing the delicate flowers, place the bouquet in a deep vase or other container until the wedding day. To preserve the bouquet, keep it well away from strong light.

ROSE PARCEL

To make a present extra special why not make the wrapping a part of the gift?
This display could not be simpler, but the finished effect is very pretty.

MATERIALS

boxed present
tissue paper
pressed flowers
handmade paper with petals
garden twine
sealing wax
3 stems roses
gift tag

TIP
Very quick and easy to make, the simplicity of this charming gift-wrap decoration is irresistible.

1 Cover the box with several layers of tissue paper. Scatter pressed flowers on the top before wrapping around the handmade paper.

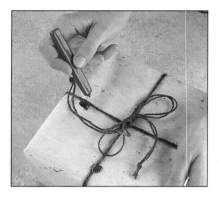

2 Tie a double length of garden twine around the parcel, then finish off with a bow. Drip sealing wax on to the string to secure it.

3 Tuck three dried roses under the twine, write a message on a gift tag and tie it on to the bow.

CHRISTMAS CANDLE POT DISPLAY

This display is designed to make the most of the rich, dark colours
of Christmas and to hint at the large variety of edible treats
we expect at this special time of the year.

MATERIALS

knife
1 block plastic foam for dried flowers
terracotta flowerpot
glue gun
stub (floral) wires
candle
hay
red amaranthus
cones
magnolia leaves
holly oak
kutchi fruit
twigs
chillies
oranges
cinnamon sticks
lavender
mushrooms
fresh moss
raffia
cutters

TIP

To create a richer look, spray the display with a clear florist's lacquer and lightly frost it with gold paint. Attach a gold fabric bow to the pot with a glue gun and replace the plain church candle with a candle that is heavily perfumed with spices.

1 Trim the foam block to fit snugly into the terracotta pot. Glue or wire the candle to the foam block. Fit the block into the pot. Wire the materials and start to push them into the foam base. Balance is very important: add the ingredients on alternate sides of the display, starting with the larger items. At this stage, the display ingredients will seem to have a lot of space between them, but as the items are added the whole design will begin to take shape.

2 Add all the smaller items – the chillies, oranges, cinnamon sticks, lavender, and so on – filling the spaces between the larger items. Trim with the moss, using a glue gun or U-shaped stub (floral) wires, so that no foam base shows. The moss can also be used to fill any large gaps between the materials, but be careful not to use too much moss or the general look will be lost. Take particular care to moss around the candle base to cover the fixings.

EVERLASTING CHRISTMAS TREE

*This delightful little tree, made from dyed, preserved oak leaves
and decorated with tiny gilded cones, would make an enchanting
Christmas decoration.*

MATERIALS

*knife
1 bunch of dyed, dried oak leaves
florist's silver roll wire
small fir cones
picture framer's wax gilt
terracotta pot, 18 cm (7 in) tall
1 small plastic foam cone for
dried flowers
4 stub (floral) wires
1 plastic foam cone for dried flowers,
18 cm (7 in) tall*

1 Cut the leaves off the branches and trim the stalks. Wire up bunches of about four leaves, making some bunches with small leaves, some with medium-size leaves and others with large leaves. Sort the bunches into piles.

2 Insert wires into the bottom end of each fir cone and twist the ends together. Gild each cone by rubbing on wax gilt.

TIP

You could make several small arrangements and then group them together to make a wonderfully festive centrepiece, or place one at each place setting.

3 Prepare the pot by cutting the smaller foam cone to fit the pot, adding stub (floral) wire stakes and positioning the larger cone on to this. Attach the leaf bunches to the cone, starting at the top with the small leaves, and working down through the medium and large leaves to make a realistic shape. Add the gilded cones to finish.

 # INDEX